A Child's First Library of Learning

Things Around Us

TIME-LIFE BOOKS • AMSTERDAM

Contents

? How Is Chocolate Made?

ANSWER Chocolate is smooth and creamy. But it's really made from beans! Cacao beans are first roasted, then made into a powder. This is mixed with milk, sugar and flavouring to make the chocolate.

■ How it grows

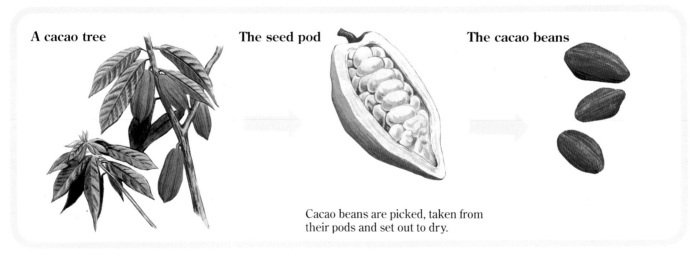

A cacao tree   The seed pod   The cacao beans

Cacao beans are picked, taken from their pods and set out to dry.

Cacao Becomes Chocolate

▲ First all the beans are washed very carefully.

▲ After that, big machines grind them into a powder.

▲ Milk, sugar and flavouring are added and the mixture is heated.

▲ The chocolate mix is poured into moulds and left to harden.

▲ Finally, the wrapper is put on. Now it's a chocolate bar!

Made from cacao

Cocoa powder, suntan lotion and face creams are some of the things we use that are made from cacao beans.

Cocoa

Cosmetics

Suntan lotion

MINI-DATA

Long ago, people living in Mexico and Central America used cacao beans as money.

● **To the Parent**

Cacao plants grow in the tropics. The countries of Ghana, the Ivory Coast and Brazil are the world's largest producers. Natives of Mexico made the first chocolate. Hernán Cortés, who conquered the Aztecs, was once served a drink made from cacao beans in the court of the Aztec ruler. He introduced the drink to Spain, but it was not till the 17th century that it became widely popular in the rest of Europe. The first milk chocolate bar was made by the Swiss in 1876.

How Is Bread Made?

ANSWER Bread is baked in an oven, of course. But many things must be done before it is ready for baking. Flour is mixed with water and yeast to make dough. The yeast makes the dough rise and keeps it soft as it bakes.

You can make bread in your kitchen. Once the dough is ready, you can pat or cut it into all sorts of different shapes. Then bake them and eat them!

■ How to make bread

▲ Mix flour, water and yeast. The dough has to be kneaded and turned over and over.

▲ Pat the dough into loaf shapes, and leave them to double in size.

▲ Put them in the oven to bake. Soon you'll have fresh bread!

Look! It's getting bigger!

Mmm, let's eat some right now!

Bakeries Make Thousands of Loaves a Day

Here's a bakery that uses machines to make all the bread. Each day it bakes 26,000 loaves. The bread goes to supermarkets and bread shops, to restaurants and also to our tables!

Bakery products

● **To the Parent**

Breads, buns and pastries come in endless varieties depending on ingredients and methods used. Most bread is made from wheat or rye flour, but other flours, such as barley or cornmeal, can be used as well. Bread made of wheat is either white or brown, rye bread is brown. Ordinary bread is made by combining yeast, salt, water and flour for the basic dough. Other breads might contain milk, sugar, butter, eggs and even honey. Pastries are made with many kinds of fillings, coatings and flavours.

❓ Why Doesn't Food in Cans Go Bad?

ANSWER Food goes bad when it's left out too long. Germs get into it, and that's what spoils the food. Germs are in the air all around us. Cans seal out air, so germs can't reach the food.

We're germs, heh heh! We make all sorts of food go bad — so you can't eat it!

Oh, oh! It's sealed — we can't find a way to get inside anywhere!

How fruit is canned

First the fruit is cleaned, then syrup is put in with it.

8

Some More Ways to Stop Food Going Bad

What's the most important thing to do to make sure food doesn't go bad? See that germs can't live around the food.

This is too dry!

Brrr! It's too cold!

Vacuum pack. This means most of the air is taken from the pack.

Dried foods. Water is taken out, so germs can't eat.

Refrigerator. It's just too cold for germs to get moving.

Salting. Lots of salt can also kill the germs.

Special containers

Some foods and drinks come in special kinds of containers. They're made of cardboard, glass, plastic and other things. Some are heated just like cans to kill germs inside.

▲ **Glass**   ▲ **Paper**   ▲ **Plastic**

The lid is sealed onto the can by a machine.

Then the cans are heated, so the germs inside are all killed.

● **To the Parent**

Ordinary cans are things that are familiar to every child. They are normally made of steel coated with tin, or of aluminium. The canning process involves preparation of the food, filling, removing air from the can, sealing, heating to sterilize, cooling and packing. You might want to show your child examples of dried, vacuum-packed, salted and canned foods found in the home. You could show them smoked, frozen and freeze-dried foods too.

? Why Does a Hard-Boiled Egg Spin Faster Than a Raw Egg?

ANSWER If you spin a raw egg the liquid inside swirls around separately. All that swirling slows the egg and throws it off balance. A hard-boiled egg's inside is solid, so its parts can't move.

TRY THIS

If you heat an egg enough, it turns hard

Ask your mother or father to heat up a frying pan, and break an egg into it. Watch how it turns hard, step by step.

▲ At first the clear part is very clear.

▲ Then it gets hotter and begins to harden.

▲ When it's really white it's all done.

Where Do Chickens Lay Eggs?

In some countries farmers keep chickens in long buildings. That makes it easy to collect the eggs they lay.

▲ These large clean buildings house many chickens. They lay eggs for people like us.

▲ See how it works inside? The eggs roll down into long trays to be picked up for market.

Eggs make many of our foods

▲ **Sponge cake**

▲ Caramel custard

▲ Madeira cake

▲ Mayonnaise

▲ Ice cream

Mmm! That looks good to eat.

● **To the Parent**

To demonstrate the difference in spins between a boiled egg and a raw egg just pick a flat surface and set both eggs spinning as you would two tops. Because the inside of the raw egg is liquid, the spin's force is not completely transmitted to its contents. Instead, the contents spin a bit more slowly than the shell, reducing overall speed. An egg white turns hard at about 80°C. The egg yolk, however, needs less heat and will begin to thicken at a temperature as low as about 67°C.

How Does Rice Grow?

ANSWER Grains of rice are actually the seeds of the rice plant. Rice is really a kind of grass. It usually grows in water, so planting and raising it is very hard work for farmers.

▲ **Rice looks like this after it's harvested**

After picking, rice stalks are used for straw.

▲ **Straw**

I am a mat made from dry rice plants cut into straw.

● **To the Parent**

Rice is recognized as one of the world's great food staples. Not only is it eaten as a cooked dish, but it is also used as the base of many other foods and condiments, and even beverages such as beer, Japanese sake and Chinese rice wine. Rice is used to make crackers, vinegar, vegetable oil and other familiar items. Wet-rice farming in paddy fields is one of the oldest forms of agriculture known and was the foundation of many great civilizations. Children will be interested to learn about the whole cycle that brings rice to their tables: planting it into seed beds, transplanting it to the fields, then irrigation, harvesting, threshing, drying and polishing. In some places, every one of these different jobs is still carried out by hand.

12

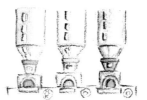

▲ Even the husks are dried and made into fertilizer.

▲ The husks on each grain are taken off by a big machine after harvesting.

▲ Next, the grains are milled. This rubs off all the brown coating, which is bran.

▲ The husks are removed to make brown rice

The rice is polished and is ready to cook

In Asia rice is even eaten on picnics

Why Does Swiss Cheese Have Holes?

ANSWER When Swiss cheese is made it is left for a long time to harden and develop flavour. A gas forms bubbles in the cheese. When it is hard the bubbles become holes.

How Cheese Is Made

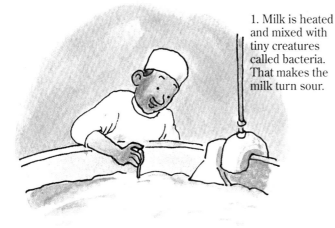

1. Milk is heated and mixed with tiny creatures called bacteria. That makes the milk turn sour.

2. The sour milk is mixed with natural chemicals and stirred until it is solid.

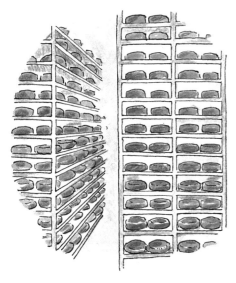

4. The cheese is removed from the moulds and left to ripen. That's when it gets its special flavour.

3. The solid pieces are cut into chunks and then put into moulds for shaping.

Some European cheeses

People everywhere eat cheese. Here are some favourite European cheeses.

● To the Parent

To make Emmenthal cheese, milk is mixed with bacteria to sour it. Rennet, a substance containing enzymes, is added to turn the sour milk into a custard-like curd. Next, salt is added and the curd is shaped in barrels or moulds. Finally, it is allowed to age or ripen. This can take a few weeks or a year. While ripening, bacteria in Emmenthal cheese release bubbles of carbon dioxide that form holes.

1. Edam, Netherlands. 2. Cheddar, England. 3. Gouda, Netherlands. 4. Parmesan, Italy. 5. Gaperon, France. 6. Cream cheese (many countries). 7. Smoked cheese, Germany. 8. Emmenthal, Switzerland. 9. Roquefort, France. 10. Camembert, France. 11. Goat cheese, France.

How Do So Many Fish Get to Market?

ANSWER We eat fish that comes from oceans, lakes, rivers and ponds. Men and women who fish bring their catch to a few big markets every day. Your local fishmonger buys fish for his shop at such a market.

Back to port

▲ Catching fish at sea

Fishing boats go out to sea to catch fish to sell. Some of them have to go a very long way, even to other countries. They're gone for months.

◄ Raising fish on farms

Some people have found a way to raise fish for food. They keep them in pools or tanks on fish farms.

Not all fish are sold in markets. Some go to factories where they are made into fish cakes, fish paste and other foods.

To market

Trucks take the fish to big markets in the city. The fish must be moved right away so they are still fresh when sold.

At the port

Fishing boats bring their catch first of all to a special market on the quayside where boats are easy to unload.

The big city markets sort out all the many kinds of fish for people who come from local shops. Your local fishmonger buys the fish there and sells them to you.

● **To the Parent**

The ocean fishing industry has two sectors: deep-sea and coastal. The deep-sea fishermen fish throughout the oceans of the world for many kinds of fish, such as cod, bonito, haddock, herring, prawns and tuna. They sell their catches to brokers at markets in their home ports who transport the fish to big wholesale centres. At these centres, fishmongers buy their stock daily for resale.

? How Are Cups and Plates Made?

ANSWER Many cups, plates and bowls are made of clay. First clay is mixed with water to make it soft. Then it is moulded into the right shape. Finally it is baked to make it hard.

OH,OH!

How pottery is made

▲ A shape is made from clay.

▲ The shapes are left to dry.

▲ Designs and shiny coats go on.

Other Kinds of Tableware

▲ Glass

▲ Plastic

▲ Wood

▲ The shapes are baked in an oven.

▲ Metal

● To the Parent

For ceramics used in the home, a special clay is mixed with substances such as mica, feldspar or silica, depending on the use and finish planned. The clay is shaped on a potter's wheel or in a press, then dried and fired in a kiln. This produces an unglazed ware such as that used for plant pots. To finish dinnerware, glaze is applied and the piece refired. Porcelain is thinner and harder than earthenware. It is translucent and rings clearly when struck.

? Where Does Electricity Come From?

ANSWER Electricity seems to come from holes in the wall, doesn't it? But it's really made by machines called generators in huge buildings called power stations. It reaches our neighbourhood through big metal wires; then it travels down into our homes to wires inside our walls.

A substation. It reduces the voltage of the electricity that comes from the power station and distributes it.

A transformer
It keeps electricity at the right voltage to use in our homes.

● **To the Parent**

Most electrical power is generated from three sources: water (hydroelectric) from dams or reservoirs; fossil fuels (oil, coal, gas); and nuclear power. The amount generated by nuclear power is growing annually. Power systems differ, but all power stations generate electricity at very high voltages, measured in kilovolts. This is reduced in local substations and again in neighbourhood transformers (often housed in their own individual little buildings) to levels we can use at home.

Dam

Hydro power station

Power lines

Thermal power station

Ways to make electricity

Electricity is made by using some other type of power to run the machinery that makes the electricity. Usually it is water from a dam; or heat from coal, oil, gas or the atom. But there are other ways, too.

Ow!

Huge windmills can drive machines to make electricity. For smaller amounts, there are little windmills, too.

You know how hot the sun is. Mirrors can collect its heat to make electricity.

Heat that comes from deep inside the earth can also be used to make electricity.

How Does a Vacuum Flask Work?

(ANSWER) A vacuum, or Thermos, flask keeps water hot in two ways. It has an inside like a mirror, which bounces heat back into the water. Behind the mirror is a space without air — a vacuum — so heat can't escape.

■ How it works

Oof! I can't get out! I just bounce back!

Hot water

Heat

The inside of the glass bottle is like a mirror, and heat bounces off it. Also, the bottle has two walls, with no air in between. Heat can't leave without air to carry it.

▲ One bottle, two walls

Some Vacuum Containers

Flasks for picnics

A rice cooker

An electric bottle

An Air-Pressure Flask

You can take water from some flasks just by pushing a button. That's because there is air inside. When you push the button, the air has nowhere to go. So it squeezes down on the water, and pushes the water out through the spout.

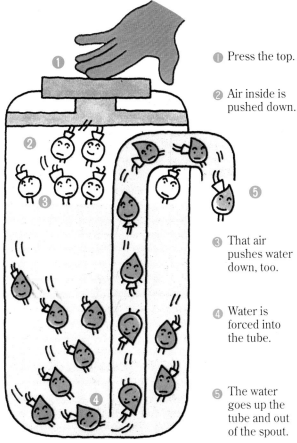

1. Press the top.

2. Air inside is pushed down.

3. That air pushes water down, too.

4. Water is forced into the tube.

5. The water goes up the tube and out of the spout.

TRY THIS

Cold things stay cold too

Fill a vacuum flask with ice-cold water and leave it. It stays cold for hours!

Wow! That's very cold!

● To the Parent

Inside a vacuum flask there is a double-walled glass jar. Its surface is metal-coated to make a mirror, which reflects the heat back inside. Between the walls there is vacuum so the heat cannot transfer to the outside. Some portable flasks have plastic or metal instead of glass, so dropping them or any other shocks won't break the flask. Vacuum flasks are normally used for liquids, but there are flasks that are made with wide mouths to carry hot or cold food.

❓ Why Does Water Put Out a Fire?

ANSWER ① For something to burn, it must be very, very hot. When water is poured on fire, the temperature drops instantly, and the fire quickly goes out.

ANSWER ② A fire also needs the oxygen in air to keep going. But there's no air in water, of course. So water keeps air away from the fire, and that's why the flames go out.

The water's too cold! I'm dying out!

Oh, I can't breathe! I'm really done for!

Air

We can also use other things to put out a fire

Air

Ooh! I can't go in there!

Powder or gas cuts off air

Containers such as this one are filled with liquid, gas or powder that doesn't burn. We spray it on the fire, and just like water it cuts off all the air. That puts out the fire, so we call the containers fire extinguishers.

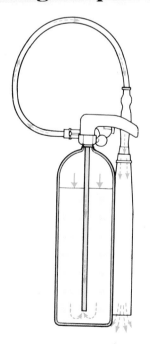

Extinguishers work in different ways. Inside this one there is a liquid. Press the button and gas pushes the liquid out of the tube. The spray smothers and cools the fire with a white foam.

I'm really glad the fire's out!

● **To the Parent**

To make things burn, high temperature and oxygen are needed. To put out a fire one or both of those elements must be removed. Water is good for fighting fire because it reduces the temperature sharply and cuts off the oxygen. It is not good for electrical fires, though, or for extinguishing oil fires because oil floats on water, so water cannot cut off the oxygen supply. So instead we use foam, powder and carbon dioxide to cut off the oxygen.

Why Do Burning Things Make Smoke?

ANSWER

When things burn, the water that was in them together with ash and tiny bits of unburnt matter form a kind of cloud. Together they make smoke.

■ When things burn...

When leaves start to burn they make a lot of smoke.

When they're burning well there's hardly any smoke.

❓ How About Fires That Don't Smoke?

Fires make a lot of smoke only when they don't burn well. The water and the little unburnt specks in smoke spread out and drift away in the air. Bigger specks fall back to the ground.

Water vapour and bits of material that didn't burn

Big specks and ashes

Help!

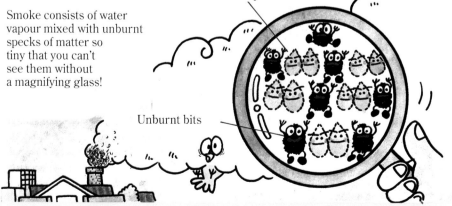
● To the Parent

In a fire the heated air sweeps water vapour, bits of the fuel that failed to burn and tiny specks of ash up into the air. The vapour itself is invisible but if it cools then it can be seen as droplets. These come together with other droplets and the unburnt bits, and make smoke. When a fire burns well, it consumes even soot, so there is not much smoke. That's why a pan won't turn as black over a hot blue flame as it will over a yellow one.

？ Why Won't Oil and Water Mix?

ANSWER Some things mix easily with water. But not oil. It weighs less than water. Instead of mixing with it, the oil floats on top of the water, as you can see below.

Water is heavier than oil. In the same jar water will sink under the oil.

You can stir and stir, but the oil will always keep to itself, even in tiny bits.

TRY THIS

Oil keeps to itself in water

Put some oil and some water into a clean glass, and watch what happens when you stir them. Even though the oil breaks up into bits, the bits won't mix with the water.

When oil meets oil, they don't have any trouble mixing with each other.

Oil and water, though, aren't the same. Those two always separate.

Water and most things with water in them, such as milk, mix very easily.

When you stop stirring, the bits of oil slowly start to move back together again.

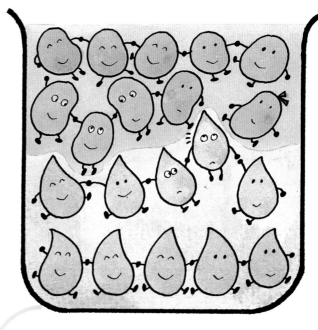

The oil rises back to the top, where it was, and soon both are separated again.

They're not very friendly!

● To the Parent

From edible oils to petroleum, oils come in various forms. You see them even in such solid fats as cheese and butter. But we generally use oil as the word for the liquid forms. Water and oil are made up of molecules that are not attracted to each other and won't link together, so oil and water do not mix. Also, oil is lighter than water, so even if you shake very hard, the oil will rise and float on the water.

Where Does Petrol Come From?

ANSWER Petrol is made from oil which is pumped out of the ground. A special chemical process separates the oil into several different parts. One of these is the petrol that is used in cars and trucks.

Petrol Comes From a Big Oil Family

Petrol is one of the many products that are made from crude oil. Each is made in its own way. These products have their own names and are used for different purposes.

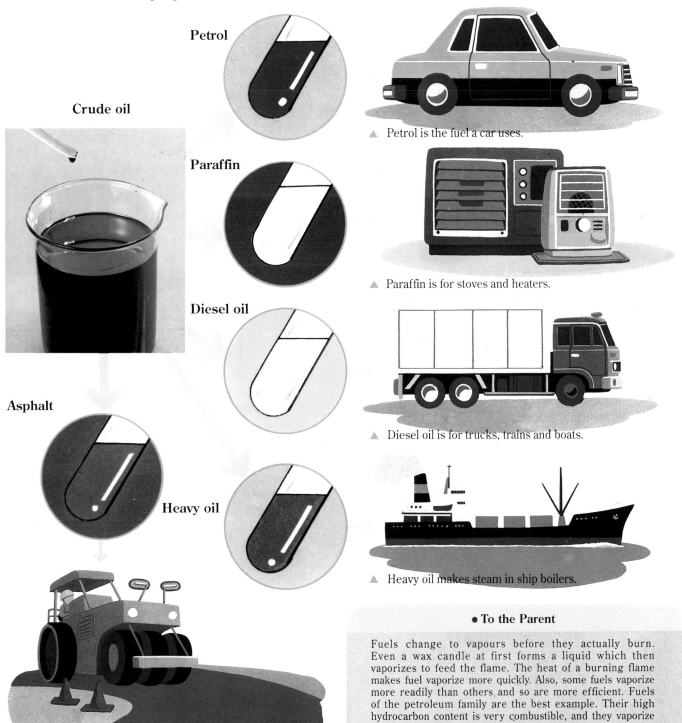

Crude oil

Petrol

▲ Petrol is the fuel a car uses.

Paraffin

▲ Paraffin is for stoves and heaters.

Diesel oil

▲ Diesel oil is for trucks, trains and boats.

Asphalt

Heavy oil

▲ Heavy oil makes steam in ship boilers.

▲ Asphalt is used to surface roads.

● **To the Parent**

Fuels change to vapours before they actually burn. Even a wax candle at first forms a liquid which then vaporizes to feed the flame. The heat of a burning flame makes fuel vaporize more quickly. Also, some fuels vaporize more readily than others and so are more efficient. Fuels of the petroleum family are the best example. Their high hydrocarbon content is very combustible, and they vaporize well. Refining of crude oil into other products takes advantage of the different boiling temperature of each product refined.

❓ Where Do They Take All the Rubbish?

ANSWER Some rubbish can be burnt, and it goes in big trucks to a special plant where they do the burning. It's called an incinerator plant. Other rubbish is taken by trucks to a rubbish dump.

The rubbish trucks come to your house on regular days to collect the things you throw away. But that's just the first step.

Some things will not burn so well

Dumping sites. Some items won't burn or are too bulky. They go to the dumping ground. In some areas, all rubbish is dumped.

Why Are Places Like This Needed Just to Burn Rubbish?

There's the truck that took our rubbish! It'll be burnt very quickly in that big building over there.

◀ **An incinerator plant**

Because the rubbish is burnt very quickly and very cleanly here there's almost no smoke, no mess and no bad smells. In fact rubbish can be very useful. The heat from burning it can be used to heat water, or for central heating.

■ How some plants work

Heat is used to make hot water

The rubbish goes in

Then it's burnt

Some ash is left

■ There are many ways the hot water can be used

▲ To fill heated pools

▲ Even for making electricity

● **To the Parent**

Not too long ago every household had to dispose of its own rubbish. Local authorities manage this unpleasant chore now. Refuse for burning is incinerated in plants at extremely high temperatures. Other rubbish is hauled away to dumps or used as landfill. Experiments have shown that resources such as metals can be extracted from both burnt and unburnt rubbish. Moreover, both can also be processed into fertilizers or fuels.

❓ How Does a Telephone Work?

ANSWER When we talk into a phone it turns the sound of our voices into an electric signal. The signal travels over wires. At the other end another phone turns it back into sound.

Telephone exchange

Hello Grandma! Thank you for the chocolate!

Electrical signals carry your voice

TRY THIS

You can make your own telephone

Use two cardboard tubes, or tins.

Cover one end with strong, thin paper and tape.

Put five metres of string through the centre and knot it tightly.

Are you there?

Of course I'm here!

To talk, pull the string tight and speak very loudly! Vibrations from your voice travel along the string.

How a telephone works

You hear the voice vibrations here

And you speak into this end

Thank you for the chocolate!

Here are some old ones

▲ 1897   ▲ 1927   ▲ 1950

▶ Public telephone booth

▲ A speaker on this office phone has a volume control.

HELLO KITTY

▲ Look at this phone!

● To the Parent

Sound is transmitted by vibrations. The telephone uses this principle to convert the vibrations of your voice into electrical signals that can travel along wire. A telephone has a small microphone in the speaking end of the handset and a tiny speaker in the earpiece. A phone call creates two circuits: microphone to speaker at each end. Many new refinements are being added, such as cordless telephones; we already talk by satellite, and soon our voices will travel on light waves.

❓ How Does a TV Work?

(ANSWER) TV signals are sent through the air as electromagnetic waves. TV aerials catch the waves, and TV sets convert them into sound and pictures.

TV aerial ▶

3. TV tower
This tower sends out the sounds and pictures as electromagnetic waves.

4. TV set
It converts the waves into pictures again by using beams to draw them all on the screen quickly.

Tiny TVs

▲ **A head-set model**

• To the Parent

Television is a complicated technology that has become part of our daily lives. The camera converts the picture into electrical signals which are then transmitted to the home from the TV station's tower as radio waves. The television tube turns them back into pictures by shooting electron beams at its screen from behind. The beams strike phosphor bits on the screen, lighting them up. The action comes from showing a series of still pictures very fast — rather like the frames of a cine film.

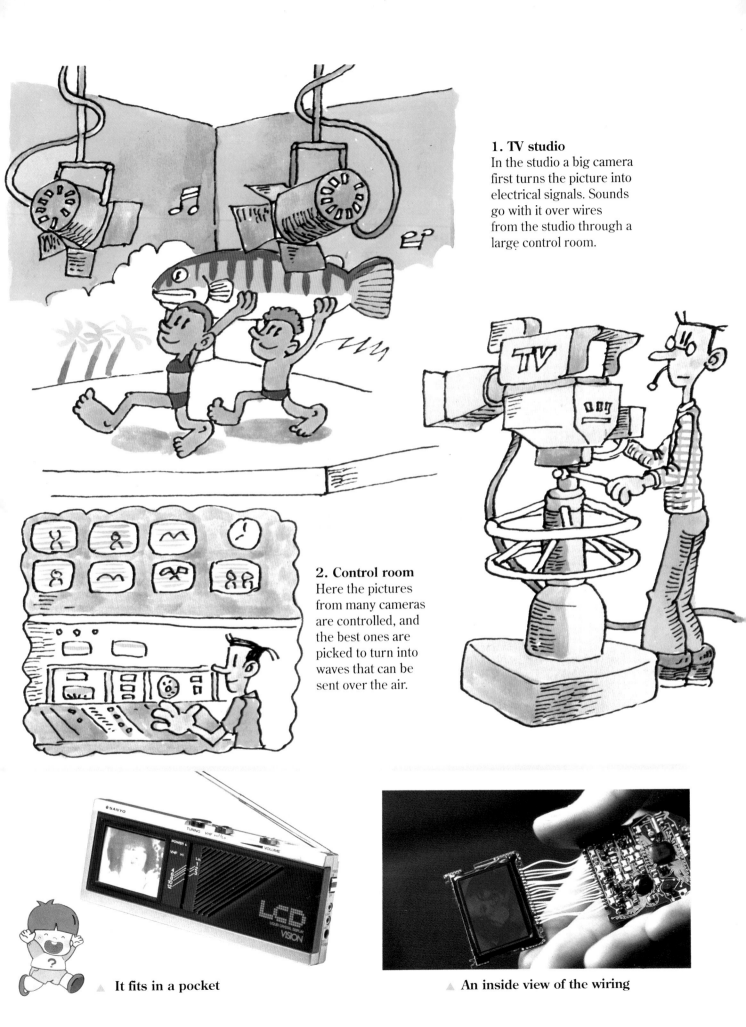

1. TV studio
In the studio a big camera first turns the picture into electrical signals. Sounds go with it over wires from the studio through a large control room.

2. Control room
Here the pictures from many cameras are controlled, and the best ones are picked to turn into waves that can be sent over the air.

▲ **It fits in a pocket**

▲ **An inside view of the wiring**

?How Does a Piano Make Music?

ANSWER Inside the piano there are lots of strings made of steel. Each time you strike a key, a little hammer hits a string. That makes the sounds.

■ Inside the piano

Strings
Different sizes, lengths and tensions make different sounds!

Hammers
Press the keys, and hammers hit the strings.

▲ The hammers are covered with felt.

■ How a piano makes notes of music

When a hammer hits a string, the string vibrates and makes a sound. That's called a note. Each string has a different size and tension, so each makes a different note. We play many notes together to make music.

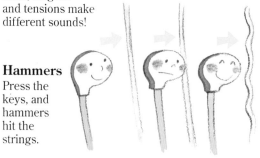

How Do Other Instruments Make Their Own Sounds?

▶ **Guitar.** These strings are strummed with your fingers.

▲ **Xylophone.** When you hit a key it vibrates to make a note.

▲ **Drum.** When the tight skin is hit it makes a noise.

▲ **Glasses.** With different water levels, their sounds differ.

◁ **Rubber band.** Twang a rubber band: it makes a funny sort of sound.

◁ **Violin.** The strings make sounds from the bow scraping on them.

▲ **Whistle.** Yours lips are the instrument through which air vibrates to make notes!

◁ **Flute.** With this, the air vibrates inside the instrument. Your fingers make the notes.

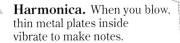

▲ **Harmonica.** When you blow, thin metal plates inside vibrate to make notes.

● **To the Parent**

Sound, as we saw with the telephone, comes from vibration. The vibration is transmitted through the air and strikes our eardrums to make them vibrate also. This is what we detect as music when we hear an instrument or song. Musical instruments are divided into various types, depending on how the vibration is made: by striking, strumming, scraping or blowing. The sound is deeper when the source (e.g. a piano string) is thick or long, and higher when it is thin or short.

? How Does a Record Make Sounds?

ANSWER If you look closely at a record you'll see many tiny grooves. These grooves contain a kind of code. A record player is made to read the code and turn it into music.

■ A record's grooves

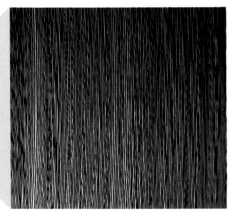

▲ A close-up look at the grooves

The lines you can see on records are called grooves. Tiny bumps on the grooves contain all the information that a record player needs to make music.

■ How a record player works

The needle of the record player is vibrated by the bumps in the grooves. These vibrations are changed into electrical signals.

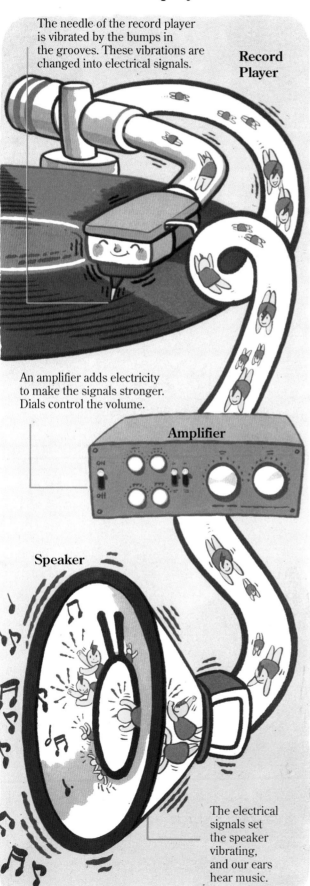

Record Player

An amplifier adds electricity to make the signals stronger. Dials control the volume.

Amplifier

Speaker

The electrical signals set the speaker vibrating, and our ears hear music.

Pictures on Records

A laser disc is like a record but it makes pictures as well as sound.

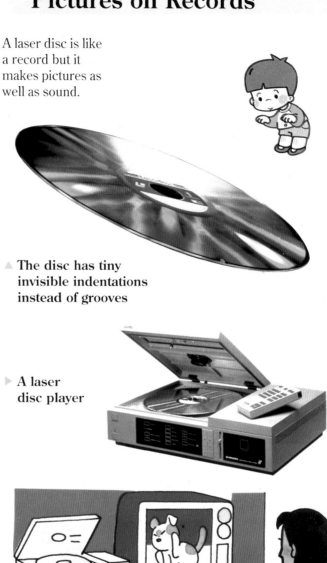

▲ The disc has tiny invisible indentations instead of grooves

▶ A laser disc player

? How Are Pencils Made?

ANSWER A mineral called graphite is mixed with clay to make pencil lead. The pencil lead is then put inside a long holder made of wood.

Making pencils

△ First, graphite is made into powder and mixed with clay. A machine shapes the mix to turn it into a pencil lead.

△ The leads are cut into pieces as long as pencils and dried. The dried leads are then baked to make them hard.

△ A long piece of wood is cut with a groove, and the lead fits right in. Another piece of wood is glued on top of it.

Pencil Leads Can Be Made Hard or Soft, Thick or Thin

Pencils with soft, thick leads make dark marks and are used to draw pictures.

Pencils that have medium softness and thickness in their leads are used for writing.

Pencils with thin, hard leads are used for technical drawings and plans.

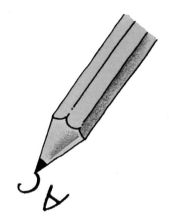
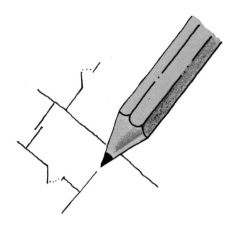

Pencils of all kinds

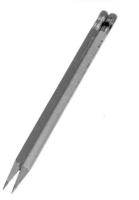

▲ Some have erasers attached

▲ Some pencils don't have graphite leads

▲ Some sets have many colours

▲ Some are made with flat points

▲ Some are made for notebooks

▲ The wood is then shaved flat or rounded smoothly on all sides, paint is added, and the pencil is finished!

Letters and designs can be added when the paint goes on.

43

How Does an Air Conditioner Cool a Room?

ANSWER An air conditioner sucks warm air into itself, removes the heat from the air and sends cooled air into the house. The heat is sent out of the house. An air conditioner is designed to do this over and over again.

Wow! It's HOT!

But not in here!

■ How air is cooled

Air conditioners use a special fluid that changes back and forth from a liquid to a gas very easily. But each time it goes back to a gas, a process called evaporation, it takes heat out of the air.

Outdoors

Indoors

Evapora

Where th liquid is made into gas again

Condenser

▲ **Where heat goes out**

Compressor

▲ **Cooling area**

What Makes the Inside of the Refrigerator Stay Cold?

A refrigerator works in a similar way. But it keeps the cold air inside. The heat is sent out through coils in the back.

Freezer section. Here's where you make ice and keep your ice cream!

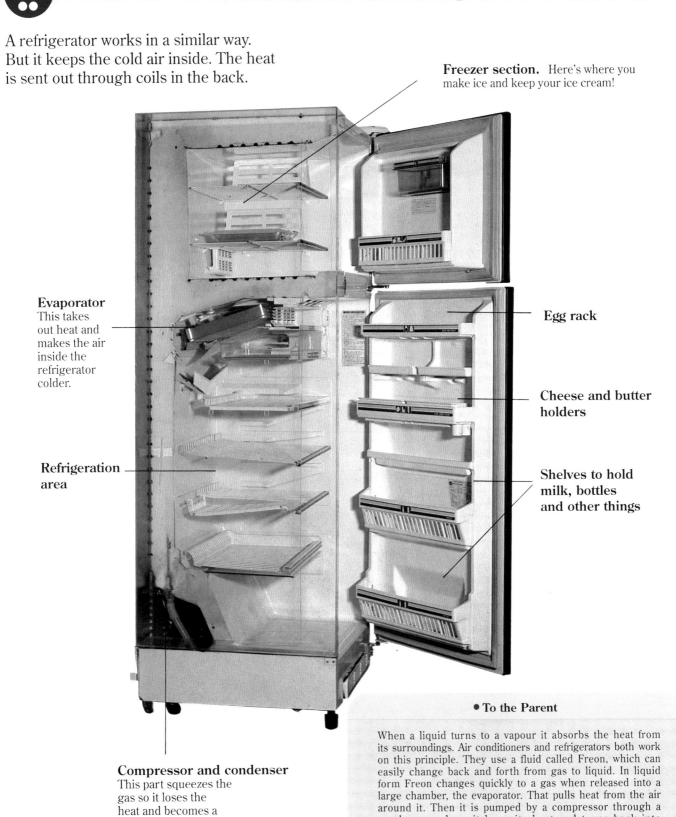

Evaporator
This takes out heat and makes the air inside the refrigerator colder.

Refrigeration area

Egg rack

Cheese and butter holders

Shelves to hold milk, bottles and other things

Compressor and condenser
This part squeezes the gas so it loses the heat and becomes a liquid once again.

❓ Why Can't We See Clearly Through Frosted Glass?

ANSWER The glass is rough on one side so light can't go straight through. If light is mixed up, the things we see are too.

I'm too small to see! What's going on?

■ How light goes through frosted glass

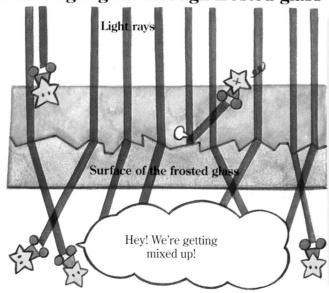

Light rays

Surface of the frosted glass

Hey! We're getting mixed up!

TRY THIS

Making frosted glass clear

Take a wet rag, and very slowly wipe the rough side of the glass so that water clings to it.

Look closely at the wet parts, and you'll be able to see! It's because the water fills in the roughness, making a flat surface again.

How do They Make Frosted Glass?

The surface of frosted glass is made rough by putting many small scratches on it. They are made by blowing tiny bits of sand at a high speed against one side of the glass.

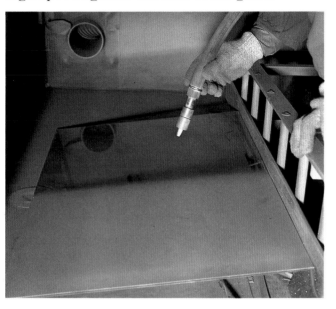

▲ This man is making frosted glass by spraying sand. The white part is already finished.

The reason some light bulbs are white is because they are frosted, too. Bulbs are treated with chemicals, however, rather than sand.

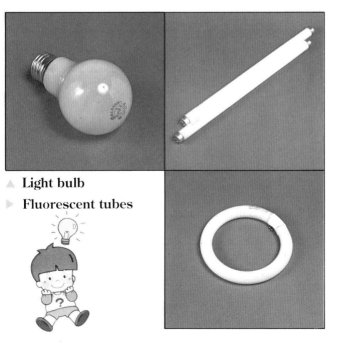

▲ Light bulb

▶ Fluorescent tubes

Many Pretty Patterns

▲ Designs can be drawn by blowing sand

▲ Coloured glass   ▲ Glass with wires

◀ Glass that looks like a mirror

● To the Parent

Transparent glass allows rays of light to pass through it without bending, and the images they carry are seen clearly. The unevenness of frosted glass directs the rays into random patterns, so images cannot be seen distinctly. Frosted glass was formerly made with tiny bits of hard sand on the surface itself, but today machines blow the sand over the surface to erode it. Light bulbs are frosted with hydrogen fluoride, a gas that corrodes glass. Fluorescent tubes are coated with phosphor.

Why Do We Stir Bath Water?

ANSWER Water on top is hotter than water down below. So we have to stir to make sure they mix well.

OH BOY! THAT'S JUST RIGHT!

YOW!! THAT WATER'S FREEZING

What happened? The hot water at the top felt good. But the rest, at the bottom, was still cold.

■ Hot and cold water

As water is heated it expands like anything else. That makes it lighter, which means it floats upwards. In baths with separate hot and cold taps, and in the Japanese bathtub here, hot water tends to collect at the top. Water that's not as hot stays heavy and sinks down to the bottom. That means that before you get in you have to stir.

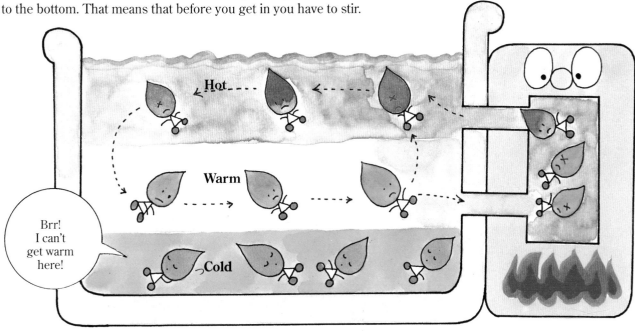

TRY THIS

Warm air gets lighter

In a room with one heater, the warm air gets lighter and goes up to the ceiling quickly. Cool air sinks down to the floor. If you stand on something high you'll feel warmer.

● **To the Parent**

When water or air are heated they expand and become less dense than an equal volume that is cold. For that reason, warm air or water weighs less than the same volume of cold air or water, and warm is pushed upwards as the cold sinks. This process is called convection, and it is why the evaporator, or cooling part of a refrigerator, is at the top. This is also the reason why an air conditioner should be placed high inside a room.

51

? Why Do Bathroom Windows Steam Up?

ANSWER The windows steam up because some of the hot bath water turns into a gas called water vapour, which floats up to the window. After a while there's so much vapour that it sticks to the glass and makes it fog up.

TRY THIS

Water drops make the glass steamy

Wipe your hand over a steamy window. Feel how cool it is.

Vapour that the glass has cooled will come off as drops of water.

■ Water vapour changes back to water when it's cool

 ANSWER 2 When water vapour gets cool it changes to tiny drops of water. The window glass is cool from outside air. It cools the vapour on the window and turns it back into water.

❓ Why Does Soap Take Dirt Out So Easily?

ANSWER Some dirt has oil in it. Water won't mix with oil. But soap mixes with both, so it lets water wash away oil.

◼ Soap pulls out dirt

▲ Soap mixes with water and finds the dirt.

▲ The soap breaks the dirt spot into tiny bits.

▲ The soap surrounds the dirt and pulls it into the water.

Oil and water mix

Most dirt will wash away with water. But not oily dirt. You can see how soap makes the oil go by mixing them in clear water.

◁ Fill a glass about half full of warm water, and put in a little salad oil. See how the oil floats on top of the water?

◁ Scrape off a few flakes of soap, put them in and stir very well.

◁ The soap breaks the oil down into tiny, tiny bits. These mix with the water, making it cloudy.

Different Kinds of Soap

■ Hand soap for your skin

■ Kitchen soap for dishes

■ Laundry soap for clothes

● **To the Parent**

Most dirt that cannot be washed away with ordinary water is oil-based; it won't mix. Soap has a chemical structure that will dissolve in water and penetrate oil to break it into very tiny bits. This both dissolves the dirt and makes the oil capable of mixing into the water so it can be flushed away. Waterfowl depend on the same oil-water principle to stay afloat. Their feathers are coated with natural oil. In soapy water they would lose the oil, become waterlogged and start to sink.

How Does a Washing Machine Clean Clothes?

ANSWER Look closely at your clothes. See all the tiny threads? Dirt gets in between them and is hard to get out. Blades in the washing machine move the clothes back and forth, so soapy water mixes in among all the threads, pushing the dirt out.

▲ **Inside a washing machine**

The blades at the bottom push soapy water and clothes round and round. The blades turn one way, then the other!

This blade spins back and forth.

▲ **The water goes round and round**

ANSWER 2 The soap you put in the washing water loosens any dirt in the clothes. Then the water can carry it away, down the drain.

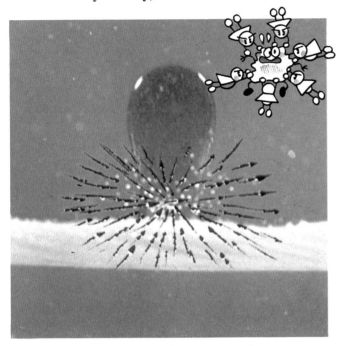

▲ Here's the soap at work. See how it surrounds a dirty spot and pulls it from the cloth?

■ Here's a BIG washing machine

This one is for a laundry and can wash a lot of clothes at one time.

Ways to Wash Clothes

▶ **Treading.** Water is poured on the clothes, and the dirt is loosened by treading on them with bare feet.

▶ **Flailing.** After clothes are soaked in water they're slapped over a rock to loosen the dirt in them.

▶ **Scrubbing.** Clothes are rubbed on a wash board in a tub of hot, soapy water to loosen the dirt.

● **To the Parent**

Oil-based dirt cannot be removed with water alone. Soap acts as a catalyst, which breaks down the oil into bits that can be washed away. Clothing has an added problem: dirt becomes trapped in the weave of the fabric and is hard to remove. Thus washing clothes has always taken a lot of hard labour. The dirt must be loosened by striking, rubbing or twisting the fabric so water can work its way in. The washing machine has made this hard process much easier.

How Do Erasers Remove Writing?

ANSWER Pencils make marks by leaving tiny bits of lead on the paper. When you rub over them with an eraser, the bits stick to the eraser and come off with it.

■ How pencil drawings are rubbed away with an eraser

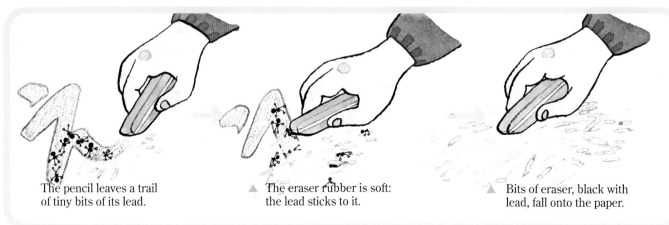

The pencil leaves a trail of tiny bits of its lead.

▲ The eraser rubber is soft: the lead sticks to it.

▲ Bits of eraser, black with lead, fall onto the paper.

But Erasers Don't Work With Things Drawn in Ink or Crayon — Why Is That?

Crayons use coloured wax to make marks, and it sticks to the paper. So erasers cannot rub it off.

Ink is a liquid, and it soaks into the paper. So rubbing the paper with an ordinary eraser won't take it out.

Types of erasers

▲ A plain eraser

▲ Erasers attached to pencil ends

▲ This eraser is shaped like a pencil

▲ Erasers with pictures

▲ Ink erasers have sand for rubbing

▲ Soft erasers used by artists

Rubber Can S-t-r-e-t-c-h and Then Shrink Back — But Why?

ANSWER Rubber is a material that stretches easily because its tiniest parts, called molecules, change shape easily. When rubber shrinks, the molecules return to their normal shape.

Take some rubber

Stretch it

Let it go

1. It starts like this.

2. It pulls in any direction.

3. Snap! It goes back to the same shape.

TRY THIS

Shooting rubber bands*

*Be sure you don't aim them at anyone!

Hold the rubber band this way

And let your little finger go!

Making rubber

▲ **Rubber trees.** If you cut the bark, a white sap, called latex, flows out. It is collected in buckets. This sap is made into many rubber products.

▲ **A tyre factory.** Chemicals are put into the sap to make it stronger. It's rolled out in big strips, then cut to make tyres.

Things made of rubber

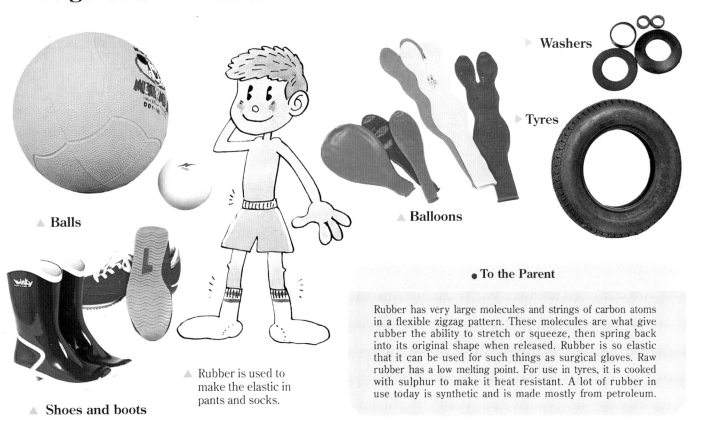

▲ **Balls**

▲ **Shoes and boots**

▲ Rubber is used to make the elastic in pants and socks.

▶ **Balloons**

▶ Washers

▶ Tyres

● To the Parent

Rubber has very large molecules and strings of carbon atoms in a flexible zigzag pattern. These molecules are what give rubber the ability to stretch or squeeze, then spring back into its original shape when released. Rubber is so elastic that it can be used for such things as surgical gloves. Raw rubber has a low melting point. For use in tyres, it is cooked with sulphur to make it heat resistant. A lot of rubber in use today is synthetic and is made mostly from petroleum.

? Why Does Steel Rust?

ANSWER Steel is very strong. But when it is exposed to air and water it will rust.

■ After a while things made of steel and iron can turn to rust

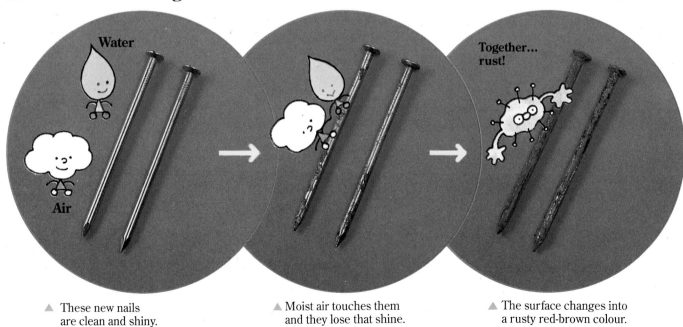

▲ These new nails are clean and shiny.

▲ Moist air touches them and they lose that shine.

▲ The surface changes into a rusty red-brown colour.

How Can We Stop Steel From Rusting?

To stop steel from rusting, we have to make sure water and air can't reach it. We can do that by painting the steel or by rubbing it with grease or oil. Or we put on a thin coat of some metal that won't rust. That's called plating.

Painting

Coating with oil

Plating. Your bicycle handlebars are made of steel. But the shiny surface is really a thin coat of chrome, another metal, which protects the steel from rust.

■ Steel that doesn't rust easily

Metals that don't rust can be mixed with steel to make stainless steel. It doesn't rust quickly.

■ This tableware is made of stainless steel

■ Some kitchen utensils are made of steel, too

■ This sink and worktop are stainless steel

● To the Parent

Rust is the result of a chemical reaction (oxidation) between the iron in steel and oxygen. Water speeds the process. Oxygen from the air dissolves in moisture on the surface, then rust starts to form. Once it starts, it continues. Untreated steel surfaces must be kept absolutely dry to prevent rust. Stainless steel resists rust because two other metals, chrome and nickel, are alloyed in it. These do not rust. That is why so many kitchen utensils are made from stainless steel.

? Why Do Magnets Attract Steel?

ANSWER Tiny iron atoms in a magnet each have a bit of electrical pull. Because they all point in one direction, they pull very strongly. Steel objects stick to the magnet because they contain iron too.

Magnets attract only metals with iron, nickel or cobalt in them. They will attract steel but not tin or lead, or non-metal objects.

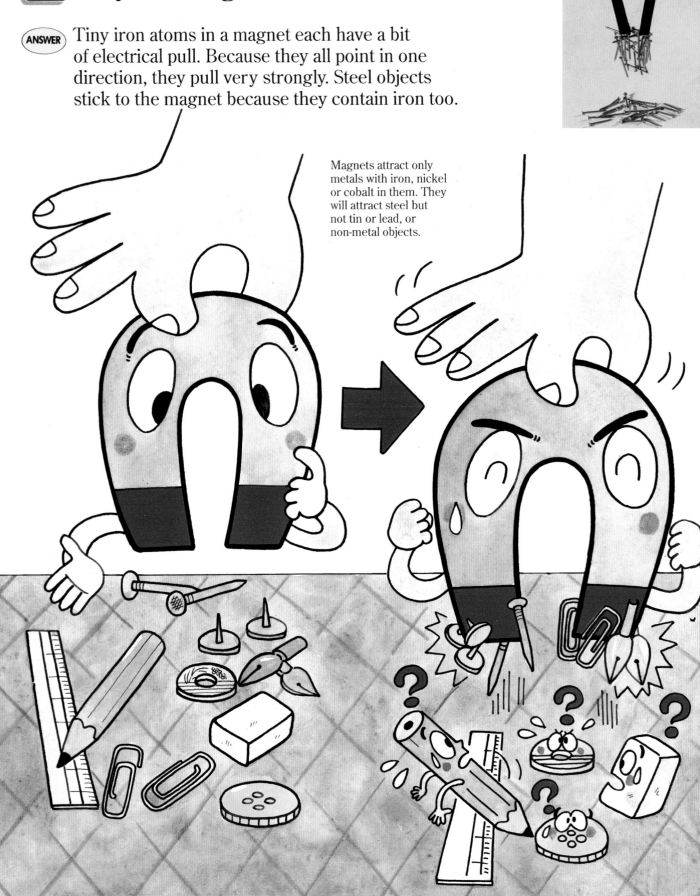

■ Steel touching a magnet acts magnetic too, so it sticks.

We've got to stick together

We are!

I've got atomic power now. Stick with me!

Hey, I'm stuck. I mean I'm not stuck! H-e-l-p!

● To the Parent

The atoms in common steel are orientated in a random fashion. But in a magnet they all point in the same direction, so their magnetic properties come into play. That is why a magnet broken in half yields not one piece with a south pole and one with a north pole, but two that have both. When ordinary steel or iron contacts a magnet, its atoms temporarily reorientate in a single direction, so the magnetism is transmitted. Nickel and cobalt act in the same way.

The Many Uses of Magnets

Magnets are used in some toys. And they are also part of important things that we use every day. Can you think of any?

Magnets make toys move

▲ Magnets hold memos

▲ Magnets close doors

▲ Magnets in board games

▲ They can stick a marker on a car

▲ This one is strong enough to lift a car

? How Does a Magnifying Glass Work?

ANSWER A magnifying glass is thicker in the centre. The thicker glass bends light before it reaches your eye, making things under the glass look bigger.

■ Why things look so much bigger

The real ladybird

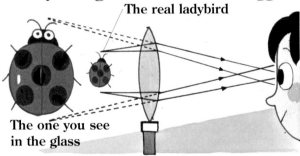

The one you see in the glass

▲ As the rays pass through the glass, they change direction, so that the eye sees an enlarged image.

● **To the Parent**

A lens is either convex (thicker in the middle), or concave (thinner). If a convex lens is held close to the eye, light rays from the object are made to converge as they pass through it, which makes the eye see a large image. Convex lenses are used in spectacles to correct farsightedness. If a convex lens is held far from the eye, distant objects appear smaller and upside down. Concave lenses make light from distant objects diverge, so they seem smaller but nearer. They correct nearsightedness.

TRY THIS

Turn things upside down

Hold the magnifying glass out. Now things far away are smaller – and upside down.

Look through nature's own lenses

Anything that we can see through, and that is thicker in the middle, makes things look bigger.

▲ **Water in a glass**

▲ **Glass marble.** If it is clear, a plain marble will make print appear larger, though it won't show much of the print.

■ Microscopes and telescopes

Both of these are to make things look bigger. Both do it with lenses.

▲ **Microscopes**
They let us look at things too small to be seen with our eyes alone.

▷ **Water flea through a microscope**

▲ **Telescopes**
They make things far away seem near to us.

❓ Why Does Soap Make Bubbles?

ANSWER Because the soap forms a film that traps air when you blow into it. If you are very careful not to blow too hard, the bubble will get very big without bursting.

■ Bubbles form when you blow air into the soap film

Water

Soap

▶ The sticky film seals itself in a ball to hold the air inside.

TRY THIS

A rainbow bubble

When you blow a soap bubble
in the sunlight you can
see a beautiful rainbow
shining on the side.

◁ If the bubble
is small it's
hard to see.

▽ But just look
at the colours
when it's big!

TRY THIS

You can blow lots of bubbles all at once

▲ Twisted wire
▽ on a straw is
all you need.

Twist lots of loops
into the wire, and
slip it into the end
of the straw. Dip it
in soap and blow!

● **To the Parent**

Soap and water will form
a thin but very strong
film. When air is blown
into this film it raises a
bubble. When the bubble
separates from the rest of the
film it seals itself through its
own surface tension. That
tension is what makes the
bubble a globe shape and gives
it its strength. As the bubble
grows larger the film gets
thinner and thinner. Rays
of sunlight are separated
as if by a prism, and that
is what makes the rainbow.

How Does Glue Work?

ANSWER 1 Wood and paper have tiny holes on the surface. Sticky glue fills in the holes. When dry, the glue holds the pieces together.

ANSWER 2 Some glues only work when two different substances are mixed together. Others, such as super-strong glue, become part of the pieces they are touching.

A kind of glue is even used between the concrete blocks of an elevated highway. Many different glues are used in making aeroplanes and cars.

Different Kinds of Glue

Ordinary glue is made from the skin and bones of animals. It's strong, but comes apart in water.

Glue made from water and plants, sometimes called mucilage, is not strong but works well on paper.

Paste made by mixing flour with water is good for hanging wallpaper.

Cement glue is made from chemicals and stays strong even in water.

❓ What Happens to Letters That We Post?

ANSWER Post office workers collect them to be sent to the people we have written to.

The postman takes the letters from the post box to the post office, where they are sorted. Other postmen deliver them.

MINI-DATA

Some of the world's post boxes

It would be a lot of trouble if we had to go to the post office each time we wanted to send off a letter, so there are boxes on the streets to put letters into. Those on the right are from three European countries.

▲ A Swedish post box

▲ A red one in Holland

▲ One used in France

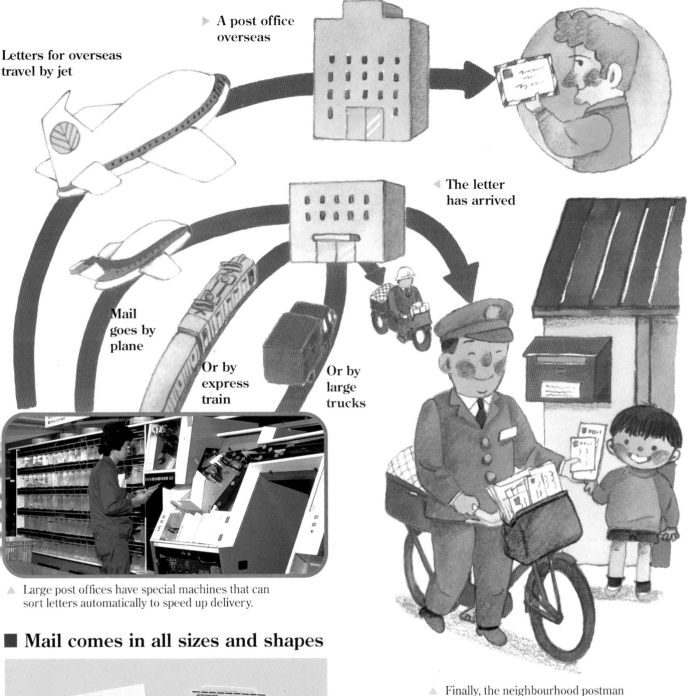

▶ A post office overseas

Letters for overseas travel by jet

Mail goes by plane

Or by express train

Or by large trucks

◀ The letter has arrived

▲ Large post offices have special machines that can sort letters automatically to speed up delivery.

■ Mail comes in all sizes and shapes

▲ Letters and cards from different countries.

▲ Finally, the neighbourhood postman delivers the letters to each house.

● To the Parent

Much modernization, such as big automated sorting machines for high-speed handling, has affected the postal service in central cities. And of course big jets now speed airmail letters to any point on the globe within days. Nevertheless, most of us think of postal service as just the handy post box or the letter slot, or the faithful postman on his daily rounds. Most countries use numerical codes for addresses to make sorting mail easier and speed up delivery.

How Does a Vending Machine Work?

ANSWER Inside the machine are large racks of the things you want. The machine counts your coins, and when you press a button it drops one of its items into a slot at the bottom.

This is a machine that sells canned drinks. The machine is cold inside, like a refrigerator.

The cold cans come out at this slot, one at a time, after you've put in the right amount of money.

The pocket in the door lets you reach into the slot and take out the can you have bought.

Down here is the refrigerator machinery. It makes sure each drink is cold when you buy it.

A Few Vending Machines

There are vending machines for almost everything. It is possible to buy newspapers and magazines, sweets, cold drinks, ice cream, washing-machine powder at the launderette, and even clothing from these machines. In places without shops, such as a park or at a bus stop, or at night when the shops are shut, they can be useful for buying small items.

◄ A newspaper vendor

This one has sweets and snacks ►

Your favourite cold drinks! ►

This one sells train tickets

◄ One for soap and bleach

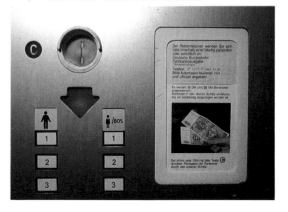

● To the Parent

Vending machines have become more familiar to us with each passing day and are now an important sector of the retail industry. They allow round-the-clock sales, they can be located conveniently close to the customer and what's more they reduce the labour costs of the retailer. Customers need not wait to make their purchases. But a growing problem in the case of beverages and foods is the disposal of empty containers. Please remind everyone not to leave litter!

❓ Why Can't a Car Always Stop Quickly?

ANSWER A moving car is pushing its weight forwards. The faster it goes, the harder the car's brakes have to work to make it stop.

TRY THIS

Run, then stop quickly

When you're walking it's easy to stop at once. But when you run it's harder.

The Faster a Car Goes, the Longer It Takes to Stop

A car moving slowly can stop quickly. One moving faster takes more time to slow down.

▶ If it's going very slowly, about 20 kilometres an hour, it can stop in only about 9 metres.

▶ A car moving at a speed of about 40 kilometres an hour takes about 23 metres to come to a halt.

▶ A car travelling at a speed of 100 kilometres an hour will run about 100 metres before it comes to a stop.

Always use your bicycle brakes safely!

A speeding bicycle will also take a longer time to stop.

▶ If you have front and back brakes use the back ones first. If you don't, you could flip over!

Be alert and brake early

● **To the Parent**

The basic laws of motion state that a moving vehicle will only slow down if acted on by a force. How quickly it slows down depends both on the vehicle and how much force is applied to it by the brakes. Thus the car's stopping distance depends not only on its initial speed and the driver's reaction time, but also on how heavy the car is and the condition both of its brakes and the surface of the road. A child's safety could depend on his or her understanding this.

❓ What Do We Have Here?

■ Tea bushes

Tea is made from the leaves of tea bushes. They are picked when they're new each spring, then steamed and dried. We put them in hot water to make tea.

■ Wood for making paper

This is a big pile of small chips of wood. They are soaked in chemicals, mashed into a kind of soup, then squeezed into thin sheets on a roller.

■ Raw plastic before it is made into shapes

To make toys and other things from it, plastic is heated until it's soft. The softened plastic is then carefully poured into moulds of toy shapes and allowed to cool.

■ Inside a music box

When you wind up the spring (1) the drum (2) begins to turn. The tiny bumps covering the drum each pluck a metal strip (3), and each makes a note!

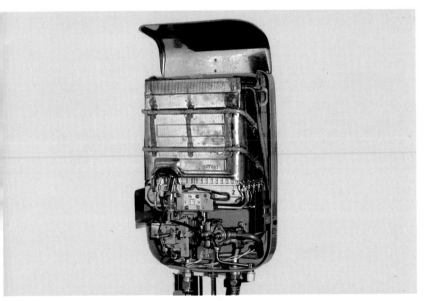

■ Inside a water heater

See the long, twisting tube? Water flows through it while gas flames shoot up from below. The water is heated from the outside as it moves along.

■ Inside an electronic game

You can't see the electricity, but you can see the screen with the figures that move. It's the square part.

● To the Parent

Black and green teas both grow on the same kind of plant, but black tea is fermented in processing. Opening up a music box is usually easy to do. But opening a water heater is extremely dangerous, and opening an electronic game case can destroy the entire game.

Do You Know What These Are?

Fire hydrant ■

Its shape is different from most hydrants that you see, but it carries water for fighting fires just like the others.

■ Electric cable

Wires like this are used for telephones, TV and other things. The colours help the workmen if the wires need some repairs.

■ Lighthouse

It's an unusual angle so you might not recognize it. Its light warns ships of dangerous rocks, so that they don't run aground.

■ Manhole cover

Many streets have pipes, sewers and cables under them. Workers go through manholes when they have to make repairs.

Growing-Up Album

Foods I Like, and Foods I Don't Like

Probably no subject in child-raising causes more controversy, and sometimes trouble, than the foods children want or refuse to eat. It is said that these preferences are learnt from parents, but that is an unproven assumption. And it is certain in any case that likes and dislikes can easily change over the years. It might be instructive to record what your child eats and then ask your doctor how well the nutritional content meets his or her growth needs.

■ **Mark the things you like with an O**
  And the things you don't like with an X

Fish

Doughnuts

Cake

Custard

Apples

Mixed lunch

Casserole

Hamburger

Bananas

Soup

Onion

Spaghetti

Sandwiches

Steak

Carrots

Pears

Eggs

Pineapple

Biscuits

Ice Cream

These are my favourite foods:

These are foods I don't like:

83

The Toys I Like to Play With Most

People and Things I See

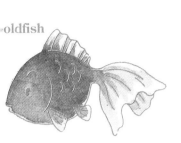

oldfish

My grandfather and grandmother

Cat

Food

My shoes

Doll

Milk

Car

People I see:

85

Here Are Some Riddles

■ The answers are all in the picture. Can you find them?

1. What has one long hand and one short hand, and moves all day?

2. What talks and shows pictures but never moves?

3. What has four strong legs but doesn't move them?

4. What do you open when you go out but never when you go in?

5. What must always take off its cap before it can go to work?

6. Where in your house is it always cold?

7. What does water go into and steam come out of?

8. What seems to get smaller as you get bigger?

1. A clock 2. A television 3. A chair 4. An umbrella
5. A fountain pen 6. In the refrigerator 7. A kettle
8. Your clothes

A Child's First Library of Learning

Things Around Us

ISBN 0 7054 1038 2
TIME-LIFE is a trademark of
Time Warner Inc. U.S.A.

Editorial Supervision by:
International Editorial Services Inc.
Tokyo, Japan

Editor:	C. E. Berry
Editorial Research:	Miki Ishii
Design:	Kim Bolitho
Writer:	Robert L. Cutts
Educational Consultants:	Janette Bryden
	Laurie Hanawa
Translation:	Ronald K. Jones

EUROPEAN EDITION:
Gillian Moore, Ed Skyner, Ilse Gray, Eugénie Romer
Editorial Production:
Maureen Kelly, Samantha Hill,
Theresa John, Debra Lelliott

Editorial Consultant for the Series: Andrew Gutelle

Typesetting by G. Beard & Son Ltd, Brighton, Sussex, England.
Printed by GEA, Milan, and bound by GEP, Cremona, Italy.

TIME LIFE CHILDREN'S LIBRARY